C900770443

WITHDRAWN FROM STOCK

## Comparing Minibeasts

# Minibeast Body Parts

## Charlotte Guillain

Raintree

you re

**www.raintreepublishers.co.uk**
Visit our website to find out
more information about
Raintree books.

**To order:**

☎ Phone 0845 6044371

🖷 Fax +44 (0) 1865 312263

📧 Email myorders@raintreepublishers.co.uk

Customers from outside the UK please telephone +44 1865 312262

Raintree is an imprint of Capstone Global Library Limited, a company incorporated in England and Wales having its registered office at 7 Pilgrim Street, London, EC4V 6LB – Registered company number: 6695582

Text © Capstone Global Library Limited 2010
First published in hardback in 2010
Paperback edition first published in 2011
The moral rights of the proprietor have been asserted.

All rights reserved. No part of this publication may be reproduced in any form or by any means (including photocopying or storing it in any medium by electronic means and whether or not transiently or incidentally to some other use of this publication) without the written permission of the copyright owner, except in accordance with the provisions of the Copyright, Designs and Patents Act 1988 or under the terms of a licence issued by the Copyright Licensing Agency, Saffron House, 6–10 Kirby Street, London EC1N 8TS (www.cla.co.uk). Applications for the copyright owner's written permission should be addressed to the publisher.

Edited by Nancy Dickmann and Catherine Veitch
Designed by Joanna Hinton-Malivoire
Picture research by Elizabeth Alexander
Production by Duncan Gilbert and Victoria Fitzgerald
Originated by Heinemann Library
Printed in China

ISBN 978 0 431 19490 5 (hardback)
14 13 12 11 10
10 9 8 7 6 5 4 3 2 1

ISBN 978 1 406 26551 4 (paperback)
15 14 13 12
10 9 8 7 6 5 4 3 2

**British Library Cataloguing in Publication Data**
Guillain, Charlotte.
Comparing minibeasts.
Body parts.

A full catalogue record of this book is available from the British Library

**Acknowledgements**
We would would like to thank the following for permission to reproduce photographs: Alamy pp. **15** (© Arco Images GmbH), **19** (© blickwinkel); Ardea.com p. **21** (© M. Watson); FLPA p. **12** (© Thomas Marent/Minden Pictures); iStockphoto pp. **13** (© Viorika Prikhodko), **22 bottom right**, **23 bottom** (© Ben Twist); Photolibrary pp. **4** (Juniors Bildarchiv), **18** (Michael Weber/imagebroker.net), **23 top** (Michael Weber/imagebroker. net); Shutterstock pp. **5** (© Ervin Monn), **8** (© photobar), **9** (© EuToch), **7** (© yxm2008), **6** (© Orlov Mihail Anatolevich), **10** (© Yellowj), **11** (© Ed Phillips), **16** (© Miles Boyer), **17** (© Miles Boyer), **14** (© Kirsanov), **20** (© David Dohnal), **22 left** (© Jens Stolt), **22 top right** (© Subbotina Anna), **23 middle bottom** (© Yellowj).

Cover photograph of ants and aphids on a stem reproduced with permission of Photolibrary (Creativ Studio Heinemann/Westend61). Back cover photograph of a spider on an iris flower reproduced with permission of Shutterstock (© Ed Phillips).

The publishers would like to thank Nancy Harris and Kate Wilson for their assistance in the preparation of this book.

Every effort has been made to contact copyright holders of material reproduced in this book. Any omissions will be rectified in subsequent printings if notice is given to the publishers.

# Contents

# Meet the minibeasts

There are many different types
of minibeasts.

head

legs

Minibeasts have different
body parts.

# Bodies

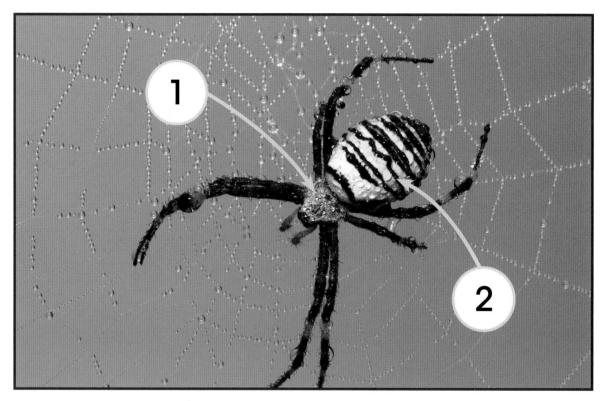

Spiders have two body parts.

Insects have three body parts.

Minibeasts do not have backbones.

shell

Some minibeasts have shells.

# Legs

legs

Insects have six legs.

Spiders have eight legs.

legs

Millipedes have many legs.

Worms have no legs.

# Wings

wings

Some minibeasts have wings.

Minibeasts use their wings to fly.

Some minibeasts use their wings to scare away birds.

Some minibeasts use their wings
to hide.

# Antennae

antennae

Some minibeasts have antennae.

antennae

Minibeasts use antennae to feel, taste, and smell.

# Stings and bites

sting

Some minibeasts can sting.

claws

Some minibeasts can bite.

Centipedes bite with claws.

# How big?

moth

ladybird

millipede

Look at how big some of the minibeasts in this book can be.

# Picture glossary

 **antenna** long, thin feeler on the head of an insect

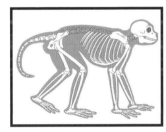 **backbone** row of bones down the middle of the back

 **insect** very small creature with six legs

 **shell** hard body covering

# Index

## Notes to parents and teachers

### Before reading

Make a list of minibeasts with the children. Try to include insects, arachnids (e.g. spiders), crustaceans (e.g. woodlice), myriapods (e.g. centipedes and millipedes), earthworms, slugs, and snails. Then ask them what body parts they think each minibeast has. Do they know how many legs each minibeast on the list has? Do they know which minibeasts have wings? What else do they know about minibeast bodies? Give the children a brief description of a backbone, what it is, and which animals have one.

### After reading

- Between spring and late summer you could go on a minibeast hunt. Put the children into groups and give each group a plastic pot, a paintbrush, and a magnifying glass. Go out into the school grounds and look under stones and leaves for minibeasts. Show the children how they can gently pick up minibeasts using the paintbrush bristles, put them into the plastic pot, then look at them under a magnifying glass. Emphasize how important it is to treat living creatures carefully and to put them back where they were found. Ask the children to try to identify the minibeasts they find and look at their body parts. Share their findings at the end of the hunt.
- Make a table to record the children's findings. Put the name of each minibeast at the top of each column and label each row with a different body part, e.g. legs, wings, antennae. For each minibeast put a tick or cross to show which body parts it has and record the number of parts if applicable.
- Remind the children that insects have six legs. Which of the minibeasts on their table are insects and which are not?